Under the Starlit Sky

For Eshan, the world is out there waiting, go out and climb it! Love, Dad – J.A.

To Bia, Tove, Ernie and Kit, for all the tree-climbing adventures to come – G.W.A.W.

The Royal Botanic Gardens, Kew carries out vital scientific
and horticultural work to protect and restore trees and forests
around the world. Kew Gardens is home to 12,000 trees including
many that are rare and endangered. Around 40,000 trees
grow at Wakehurst, Kew's wild botanic garden in Sussex.

BIG PICTURE PRESS

First published in the UK in 2025 by Big Picture Press,
an imprint of Bonnier Books UK
5th Floor, HYLO, 105 Bunhill Row,
London, EC1Y 8LZ

The authorised representative in the EEA is
Bonnier Books UK (Ireland) Limited.
Registered office address:
Floor 3, Block 3, Miesian Plaza
Dublin 2, D02 Y754, Ireland
compliance@bonnierbooks.ie
www.bonnierbooks.co.uk

1 3 5 7 9 10 8 6 4 2

ISBN 978-1-80078-737-7

This book was typeset in Adobe Caslon Pro,
Baskerville and Magilio.
The illustrations were created with pencil
and coloured with watercolour.

Edited by Matt Ralphs and Russell McLean
Designed by Winsome d'Abreu and
Melissa McInerney
Paper engineering by Richard Ferguson
Production by Neil Randles

Printed in China

Under the Starlit Sky

James Aldred

Illustrated by
**Good Wives
and Warriors**

Royal
Botanic
Gardens **Kew**

Białowieża Forest

Straddling the border of Poland and Belarus, the Białowieża Forest World Heritage Site is the last remaining fragment of a vast, ancient **ecosystem** that once covered most of lowland Europe. Home to wolves, bison, elk and boar, this is the original wild wood – a place of myth and legend, folklore and fable. A tangled realm of ancient trees, impenetrable wetlands, and secret wildflower meadows where 50-metre-tall trees tower above those who venture in.

A forest has stood here since the end of the last ice age. For almost 12,000 years, ever since the first pioneering plants took root in the wake of the retreating ice sheets, trees have grown, fallen and died here, enriching the soils and creating one of the world's most complex and **biodiverse** ecosystems. A unique place of infinite variety and natural wonder where new **species** are still being discovered almost every year.

Białowieża Forest is beyond precious. It is the beating heart of **primeval** Europe. A window on the past through which we are still learning important lessons for the future.

60m

Upper canopy

40m

Canopy

20m

Understory

Brushwood layer

Herb layer

0m

Forest floor

A Forest Adventure

Like every forest, Białowieża is defined by its trees. They are the framework upon which the entire ecosystem depends. Even in death, these giants provide food and shelter for countless **organisms**. But what we see from the ground is barely a fraction of the story. The real action takes place high above us, hidden from sight within the vast network of branches and leaves that forms the biological **interface** between our planet and beyond. It is up there, above the gloom of the forest floor, where the sun's energy first enters the ecosystem via the chemical process of **photosynthesis**. And it is up there we must venture if we are to fully appreciate the way in which everything is connected.

Białowieża Forest is a huge, ancient, living entity in which energy moves continuously up and down between canopy and soil. We will make this same journey using ropes and harnesses to climb up from the ground, immersing ourselves in each of the forest's layers as we ascend. By the time we return to the ground we will have a much greater understanding of how the forest works, and the vital roles that even the tiniest plants and animals play in the bigger picture.

Białowieża is home to many giant trees. One of the biggest and oldest is the mighty Maciek oak. Four and-a-half-centuries old, this 41-metre-tall veteran will be our guide as we climb into its branches for a unique view of the forest. It won't be easy, but nothing worthwhile ever is. So, grab your harness, helmet and rope . . . and let's get climbing!

Mycorrhizal Network

In ancient forests, **fungus** roots intertwine with plant roots to form webs known as **mycorrhiza**, which can connect hundreds of trees. The fungi receive food from sap carried in plant roots; in return, plants receive minerals that only the fungi can absorb from the soil. Trees also share **nutrients** and transmit chemical messages to each other via the mycorrhizal network.

Fly Agaric Mushrooms

These striking toadstools pushed their way up through the leaflitter under cover of darkness. The **fruiting bodies** produce dust-like **spores** that float away on the wind to grow into the next generation elsewhere in the forest. Be careful not to touch this fungus – it may be beautiful, but it is also poisonous!

Fungal Mycelium

These fine fluffy threads are called '**mycelium**' – the roots of fungi. Fungi are not plants. Neither are they animals. Capable of growing far bigger than the largest tree, they can spread through the soil for tens of metres in every direction. They break down and gather rare nutrients and minerals using chemical **enzymes**.

The Forest Floor

Sooner or later, everything living in the forest's upper layers ends up back down here. Even the mightiest trees eventually die, returning to the soils from which they grew. But this is not the end. In fact, it is just the beginning, because this rich organic material is slowly broken down and turned back into food for the next generation of living things. The earth is a recycling powerhouse – packed full of countless organisms, all busily converting yesterday's dead material into tomorrow's life-giving energy.

A rich, musty aroma rises as you kick through the leaves on your way to the tree. Beneath your feet lies a secret, mysterious world inhabited by millions of microscopic organisms. By walking through the forest you have become part of its vast, ancient ecosystem. Each footstep is felt by countless other living things.

Dor Beetles

These dor beetles are busily digging burrows beneath a bison cowpat. Females lay eggs on rolled pellets of dung stored at the end of each tunnel. After hatching, beetle grubs feast upon faeces before pupating into adult beetles, ready to begin the cycle again.

Bumble Bee Nest

A queen bumble bee sways gently as she flies over the **leaflitter** in search of a safe place to nest. Once she's chosen – an old mouse burrow, perhaps – she will lay eggs in the cosy chamber. She keeps them warm with her fur, waiting for her daughters to hatch as she sips flower nectar from a wax pot beside her.

Germinating Acorn

This acorn fell from the branches of its parent last autumn. With the arrival of spring, the hard protective shell has split. A delicate shoot pushes up into the light; a thread-like root worms down into the soil. This tiny capsule of life may one day grow into one of the largest living things in the forest – a mighty oak.

Woodlice

Closely related to sea-dwelling shrimp, these **crustaceans** breathe through gills and live in moist, dark places. Mothers keep their newly hatched offspring safe inside pouches. But what makes them really special is the role they play in recycling forest nutrients: rotting wood, soggy leaves, poisonous fungi, dead animals and poo are all on the menu. Yummy!

Earthworms

The lowly earthworm is one of nature's unsung heroes! At night, they drag fallen leaves and other dead material into their burrows to feed on. The waste they leave behind is rich in nutrients that would otherwise remain inaccessible to other organisms.

Tree Roots

Over countless years, the roots of ancient trees twist slowly through the soil, providing essential support and stability. They also play a vital role in resource gathering. The massive roots divide into complex networks of hair-thin fibres until – at their very tips where surface area is at its greatest – they absorb water, minerals and nutrients from the surrounding soil.

Herb Layer

Unlike tropical rainforests such as the Amazon, which are bathed in 12 hours of warm sunlight every day of the year, forests in the north make do with a much shorter growing season. Winter comes early and stays long. Białowieża is often covered with snow for three months every year. Daylight hours are short, and winter temperatures plummet to -30°C. Streams freeze, and the forest is ice-locked for weeks on end. But something magical happens when spring arrives, and with only around 150 days to flower, fruit, grow and reproduce, the race is on!

Around 450 years ago, an acorn germinated on this spot. Growing slowly up through the fallen branches of its dying parent, by the time it was 30 years old it was safely beyond the reach of browsing deer. Now, it rises more than 40 metres into the canopy. This is the mighty Maciek oak, the biggest in the forest. And as you peer up its tall, straight trunk, you realise that you have a very long climb ahead!

Wildflowers

Even before the last of the snow has melted, spring's first flowers send delicate green shoots up from deeply hidden **bulbs** and **rhizomes**. Within weeks, there is a green haze of fresh **foliage**. A riot of colour follows as hundreds of thousands of flowers open vibrant petals to attract bumble bees, butterflies and other insect **pollinators**. By early June, the spring flowering is over for another year!

Eurasian Woodcocks

A female woodcock sits low on a nest, incubating her eggs as her mate probes for worms in the soil with the flexible tip of his long beak. These secretive, perfectly **camouflaged** waders have almost 360-degree vision to warn them of approaching danger.

Wood Ant

This heaving pile of twigs and spruce needles is actually a wood ant nest, home to 400,000 sister workers busy **foraging** and moving debris around to maintain a constant, warm temperature. Much of their vast home is hidden underground, and somewhere down there lies their queen, whose job is to lay hundreds of eggs every single day. The workers protect her and their home by spraying formic acid from their abdomens at intruders!

Rhino Beetle

This large white grub is the immature **larva** of a rhino beetle. Safe inside a decaying fallen tree, it uses powerful crunching jaws to feast on the rotting wood previously broken down by fungi. It will spend up to three years in here before pupating and emerging as an adult.

European Bison

Białowieża is one of the last remaining strongholds of the European bison, Europe's largest native land mammal. Signs of them are everywhere. From the deep, cloven hoof prints in the muddy banks of streams, to the steaming piles of fresh dung so loved by insects, these are true architects of the forest, fertilising the soil and keeping it free from undergrowth.

Cauliflower Fungus

This spectacular cauliflower fungus consumes living tissue. Over time, it breaks down lignin and cellulose, the woody substances that give trees their strength. Some trees survive for decades, others succumb quickly, but sooner or later the tree will die and return to the leaflitter – a feast for the organisms in the soil.

Wild Boar

Wild boar use their strong yet sensitive snouts to root for food. They eat almost anything: worms, insects, fungi, flower bulbs, rodents, bird eggs – even dead animals. By churning and aerating the ground, boars mix the soil and help seeds to germinate. With poor vision, they rely on a keen sense of smell, and as one lifts its head to taste the air, you catch a glimpse of its formidable tusks. Maybe it can smell you!

Norway Spruce Seedlings

These spruce seedlings have taken root on a fallen tree. Safely above the reach of deer, boar and bison, they push up into the light gap created by the fallen tree. Moss provides their roots with water, whilst nutrients are absorbed from the decaying wood. By the time this nursery log crumbles away, the spruces will be large enough to support their own weight.

Small-Leaved Lime Tree

Protected from hungry deer and bison by the surrounding fallen timber, this young lime tree is safely above the browse line: the maximum height that herbivores can reach. Its tender leaves are beyond even the tallest elk, but still provide food and cover for many smaller creatures.

Northern Eurasian Lynx

Supreme predators, lynx need large territories in which to live – Białowieża is home to around 40 individuals. They hunt birds and mammals, from small rodents to wild boar and young elk. This one leapt onto a roe deer's back, killing it with a bite to the neck before dragging the carcass onto a fallen tree, out of the reach of wolves that would not only steal its food but also kill the lynx.

European Tree Frogs

European tree frogs call from a leafy branch with strange, rhythmic croaks. Their inflated throat sacs show that these are males singing to attract mates. If successful, the female will lay her eggs in rain-flooded root hollows left by toppled trees.

Carpenter Ant

With queens as long as a paperclip, carpenter ants are Europe's largest ants. This colony has made a home inside a fallen spruce. By chewing away the soft summer wood between the hard growth rings of winter, they have created a network of tunnels and chambers for raising their young.

Brushwood Layer

Large areas of Białowieża remain untouched by humans. Unlike commercially managed forests where deadwood and wind-blown timber is often cleared away, here it lies where it falls. Such debris provides shelter and food for countless insects, fungi and **epiphytes**. In turn, these support large, diverse populations of birds and small mammals, as well as the **predators** that feed on them. Deadwood is key to a healthy forest ecosystem and high biodiversity.

Taking a rest from climbing, you spin slowly round on your rope to take a look at your new surroundings. The air feels less muggy, and a cloud of tiny stingless bees buzz around you to lick salt from your sweat-soaked t-shirt.

Eurasian Sparrowhawk

A pile of discarded feathers reveals that these woods are home to a pair of sparrowhawks. Small but deadly hunters, they often bring **prey** to the same place to pull out feathers prior to eating. These plucking posts are a record of which birds the hawks are targeting: thrushes, blackbirds, robins, tits and finches.

Eurasian Wren

This wren hunts for spiders, grubs and insects amongst the fallen timber. Males build several domed nests and females chose their favourite to lay eggs in. A single male can have three or four active nests, all belonging to different females.

Yellow-Necked Mouse

Yellow-necked mice are excellent climbers, foraging for seeds, nuts and berries high amongst the branches at night. This one is looking for a tasty fungus lower down, but it had better be careful: small rodents are on the menu for many predators, including owls.

Mosses and Ferns

Mosses, ferns and bryophytes don't grow very tall. Instead they grow as epiphytes upon the surface of larger plants. Deep tree trunk crevices and the rotting wood of fallen branches are perfect. By soaking up and storing rainwater like a sponge, they create ideal conditions for damp-loving slugs, snails and woodlice.

Understory

Not as tall as the ancient oaks and limes that tower above all, these hornbeams, elm and maple trees form a leafy understory of dense foliage and interconnected branches. Large, juicy leaves, plentiful seeds and sugar-rich bark make this one of the most energy-rich **habitat** layers in the forest. Well beyond the reach of large ground-based herbivores such as deer, this middle canopy zone is the realm of **arboreal** (tree-dwelling) animal acrobats and flyers.

Squeezing through the tangled branches of the understory, you enjoy the sensation of being immersed in dense foliage as you climb ever up towards the high canopy still out of sight above. This middle zone is a secret place; you have entered a magical, floating world where the smell of the earth is replaced by that of fresh leaves. The scent of honeydew and nectar hang enticingly in the air around you.

Aphids

Aphids use their hollow mouth parts to suck up sugary sap like milkshake through a straw. When an ant strokes an aphid's back, the bug waves its bottom in the air and produces a little bubble of sweet honeydew. This is gobbled up by the waiting ant. In return, ants protect the aphids from other predators.

Wood Ants

Wood ants make an epic climb into the understory to collect honeydew. They drink the liquid then climb back down to regurgitate it for others in their nest – a round-trip of seven kilometres in human terms. Most make this journey several times a day – the equivalent of you or I carrying a heavy backpack up and down Mount Everest twice a day!

Pygmy Owls

At less than 20 centimetres tall, the secretive pygmy owl is Europe's smallest owl. They use their unusually large feet to carry away rodent prey up to a third of their own size. This pair are nesting in an abandoned woodpecker hole high up in a dead spruce tree.

Red Squirrel

Small and light, red squirrels are the ultimate parkour experts. And they have to be, since they are the favourite item on the menu for several top predators. Most famous for their love of eating nuts in autumn, they also take eggs and small chicks from birds' nests, and eat the sugary bark of young trees in winter.

Black Woodpecker

Europe's largest woodpecker loves to eat carpenter ants. It catches them with its long tongue after it has chipped away tough deadwood with its powerful beak. This woodpecker is a vital – or 'keystone' – part of this habitat because other birds and animals use their abandoned nest holes to live in.

Honeysuckle

The heavy scent of this flowering honeysuckle advertises its sweet nectar to insect pollinators. Adored by night-flying moths, the flowers also attract small arboreal mammals such as dormice that nibble them as a tasty midnight snack.

White Admirals

White admiral butterflies lay eggs only on honeysuckle leaves. The emerging caterpillars grow through five stages of development (called 'instars'), before pupating within their elaborate **chrysalis** the following spring. The adult butterflies emerge to feed on bramble blossom and honeydew, before flying up through the canopy in search of a mate.

Northern Goshawk

This female goshawk is feeding scraps of meat to her three newly hatched chicks. These large, powerful hawks are the ultimate predator: agile, swift and relentless in pursuit of prey. They will hunt and eat anything they can catch and kill, but what this pair really loves to eat are squirrels!

Upper Canopy

The upper canopy is the highest level of the forest.
It's a powerhouse of energy, where most photosynthesis (the
process of green plants converting light energy into chemical
energy) takes place, and where the sun's energy first enters the
forest ecosystem. Billions of leaves are angled towards the sun to
take full advantage of northern Europe's short growing season.

*Having threaded your way up through the lush understory, your
climbing rope leads you into an open, sky-vaulted space inhabited
by forest giants. Standing all around, these massive trees stretch up
into the clear, starlit sky. Swaying on your rope, you feel the mighty oak
heave in the breeze as you peer at the far-reaching views. The ground
is now far out of sight beneath the dense understory below.*

Greater Noctule Bats
Greater noctule bats are true forest dwellers,
requiring old tree cavities to roost in. With
a wingspan of almost 50 centimetres, they are
Europe's largest bat and the only species known
to hunt small birds on the wing. With large
vampire-like teeth, these mysterious bats
are secretive and poorly understood.

Purple Emperors
Purple emperor butterflies defend treetop
territories by chasing off male rivals
whilst flashing their beautiful wings in
the sun to attract females. Living most of
their adult lives in the upper branches of
oaks, emperor females lay eggs on willow
bushes closer to the ground and in wetter
parts of the forest.

Black Storks
A loud clacking of beaks draws your attention to a pair of
black storks. They recently arrived from their wintering grounds in
Africa, and the male has brought fresh foliage for the nest. They
will soon lay eggs and raise their chicks on food gathered in nearby
wetlands and marshes. In this way, black storks connect a variety
of different habitats within Białowieża and beyond.

European Mistletoe

Although this mistletoe's green leaves produce food via photosynthesis, its roots run deep within its host tree to steal water and minerals. In this way, these 'hemi-parasitic' plants can inhabit the highest branches where there is plenty of sunshine, and protection from hungry mammals.

Pine Marten

Hunting squirrels is not easy if you can't fly. It takes great speed, agility, balance and an ability to leap long distances between branches. Luckily, pine martens have all these skills in abundance. Supreme acrobats, these determined hunters also eat a huge variety of other foods including eggs, birds, mice and frogs.

Oak Apple Gall

What looks like an apple growing on the oak branch is actually a 'gall'. Galls are a deformity caused by another organism, often an insect, which uses special chemicals to alter the plant's cells. This gall has been caused by a tiny wasp that lives in the soil far below. It has been created to provide a safe place for her larvae to grow and **pupate** in.

Lesser Spotted Eagles

Just like the black stork, these lesser spotted eagles migrate to central Africa each year to escape the harsh northern winter. **Apex predators**, they are raising their single chick on reptiles, amphibians, birds and mammals. Three eggs were laid in this nest, but the first chick to hatch grew quickly and killed and ate its smaller brother and sister.

Lime Leaves and Spruce Needles

These two leaves look different, but are both designed to convert sunshine into energy. The heart-shaped lime leaf falls to the ground in winter, while the smaller spruce needle stays on its tree for years. The broad canopies of lime trees and oaks are good at catching light when the summer sun is high in the sky. The tall witch-hat shape of the spruce allows its sides to absorb light even in the depths of winter when the sun is low.

A Note from the Author

Today, the Białowieża Forest is made up of two different national parks: Białowieża NP (in Poland) and Biełavieskaja Pušča NP (in neighbouring Belarus). Both parks are connected, and both countries work together to ensure they continue to be protected. The whole biome was made a UNESCO World Heritage Site in recognition of its uniqueness. As such, it has held the highest level of protection for more than 30 years.

Yet, incredibly, the Białowieża Forest biome is still being logged for profit. In 2017, around 170,000 trees were felled on the Polish side alone. Many were taken from old-growth areas despite pleas from UNESCO and the World Wide Fund for Nature (WWF) to stop.

So how and why is this still being allowed to happen?

Well, much of Białowieża sits outside the two national park boundaries. These outlying areas are still a World Heritage Site, but the logging industry has a powerful voice. After all, many people rely on it for their livelihood. It is a complex situation that occurs in many countries. It is easy to protect somewhere if there is no demand for its resources, but as trees become less available elsewhere the pressure to log within protected areas grows. This means that governments are placed under pressure to open them up for exploitation.

Many years ago, I drove my old car all the way from England to Białowieża to see the famous forest for myself. I quickly fell under its spell. For five weeks I trekked, camped, climbed trees and filmed wildlife. I watched herds of bison grazing in the meadows, filmed wild boar feasting on acorns beneath giant oaks and even saw my first wolf! It is like nowhere else on Earth, and I was struck by just how much the people who live there love and respect it. I believe that this is the key to conservation – people protect the places they care about most.

So why not visit Białowieża for yourself? It's easy to get to and YOU might be the voice who makes all the difference in helping to save it and other forests like it as they become even rarer in the future!

Glossary

Apex predator – An animal that kills other animals for food, and which is not normally hunted by other animals.

Arboreal – Living in trees.

Biodiverse – Having many different types of plants, fungi and animals.

Bulb – The round root of some plants, from which the plant grows.

Camouflage – When an animal adapts itself so that it can blend in with its surroundings.

Chrysalis – The hard case that protects an insect pupa.

Crustacean – A type of animal that lives in water and has a hard outer shell.

Ecosystem – All the living things in an area, and the way in which they connect to each other to form a community.

Enzyme – A chemical that speeds up a process in the body of a plant or animal.

Epiphyte – A plant that grows on the surface of a larger plant.

Foliage – The leaves of a plant or tree.

Forage – To search for food over a wide area.

Fruiting body – The part of a fungus that produces spores. Mushrooms and toadstools are fruiting bodies.

Fungus – A type of organism that is neither a plant nor an animal, and which gets its food from decaying matter.

Habitat – The home of an animal, plant or fungus.

Interface – An area where two different things join together and affect one another.

Larvae – Young insects after they have hatched but before they have become adults.

Leaflitter – Decomposing and dead leaves that fall to the forest floor.

Mycelium – The fine, branching, root-like threads of a fungus.

Mycorrhiza – A fungus that forms a partnership with the roots of a plant so that both organisms can share nutrients.

Nutrients – Substances that are essential for an organism to survive and grow.

Organism – A living thing

Photosynthesis – The way in which a plant uses water, sunlight and carbon dioxide from the air to produce food.

Pollinator – An animal that transfers pollen between plants, allowing fertilization to take place.

Predator – An animal that preys on other animals.

Prey – An animal that is hunted by a predator.

Primeval – Ancient.

Pupate – When an insect larva turns into a pupa. As a pupa, the insect is protected by a hard case called a chrysalis and does not move.

Rhizome – A thick stem of some plants. It grows horizontally just under the ground and produces roots and shoots.

Species – A group of plants, fungi or animals that share similar characteristics. Animals of the same species can breed with one another.

Spore – A cell produced by fungi and some plants (mosses and ferns, for example) that can develop into a new organism.

The Maciek Oak

From the humblest earthworm to the mightiest bison, the towering Maciek oak has sheltered and nourished countless animals, plants and fungi for nearly half a millennium. The wildlife we have observed on our epic climb from the forest floor to the upper canopy represents a mere fraction of all the species that call Białowieża home. There are more than 1,000 types of plant, over 3,000 fungi, 59 mammals, 13 amphibians, seven reptiles and – incredibly – more than 250 bird and 12,000 invertebrate species. Quite simply, it is one of the richest ecosystems on Earth.

SPOTTER'S GUIDE

1. *Lesser spotted eagle*
2. *Greater noctule bat*
3. *Black stork*
4. *Purple emperor butterfly*
5. *Oak apple gall wasp*
6. *European mistletoe*
7. *Pine marten*
8. *White admiral butterfly*
9. *Honeysuckle*
10. *Northern goshawk*
11. *Pygmy owl*
12. *Black woodpecker*
13. *Eurasian sparrowhawk*
14. *Carpenter ant*
15. *Red squirrel*
16. *Eurasian wren*
17. *Yellow-necked mouse*
18. *European tree frog*
19. *European bison*
20. *Fly agaric mushrooms*
21. *Wood ant*
22. *Dor beetle (rolling dung)*
23. *Northern Eurasian lynx*
24. *Cauliflower fungus*
25. *Wild boar*
26. *Eurasian woodcock*
27. *Dor beetle (laying eggs)*
28. *Woodlouse*
29. *Earthworm*
30. *Bumble bee*

19.

20.

21.